RICHARD MCLEAN

Teacher Jokes

Over 350 jokes your students will love

To mr cox, this is to help you get new jokes next year. Love Rainbow.

Copyright © 2024 by Richard McLean

All rights reserved. No part of this publication may be reproduced, stored or transmitted in any form or by any means, electronic, mechanical, photocopying, recording, scanning, or otherwise without written permission from the publisher. It is illegal to copy this book, post it to a website, or distribute it by any other means without permission.

First edition

*This book was professionally typeset on Reedsy.
Find out more at reedsy.com*

Contents

Introduction 1
Teacher Jokes 2

Introduction

This is a joke book in its simplest form.

Jokes that your students will love and nothing else.

All jokes are clean, fun, easy to understand, and perfect to grab your students' attention.

The jokes are not ordered in any way, so you have no idea what you're about to read next.

Open up wherever you like. You're guaranteed to get some laughs and soon you'll be the funniest teacher in school!

Teacher Jokes

Before you begin, we openly admit that you might think some jokes in this book are terrible. But one person's terrible is another person's hilarious. Remember that.

Why do underwear tell bad jokes?
They're too brief.

How do new pilots learn to fly?
They just wing it.

What do you call a droid that likes taking the scenic route?
R2-Detour.

Why are all of Superman's costumes tight?
They're all size S.

Why did the teacher draw on the window?
Because he wanted his lesson to be very clear.

Why does Peter Pan fly around so much?
He Neverlands.

TEACHER JOKES

What do you call a boomerang that doesn't come back?
A stick!

What did one wall say to the other wall?
"I'll meet you at the corner."

What did the zero say to the eight?
"Nice belt!"

How did Darth Vader know what Luke was getting for Christmas?
He had already felt his presents.

How much did the pirate pay for his peg and hook?
An arm and a leg.

What did the limestone say to the geologist?
"Don't take me for granite!"

What is a possum's favourite movie?
Mission Impossumble.

Why didn't the dinosaur ride the roller coaster?
She was a nervous rex.

Why did the puppy get great grades in class?
He was the teacher's pet.

What do you call a witch who lives on a beach?
A sand-witch.

TEACHER JOKES

Where should you go if you want to learn how to make ice cream?
Sundae school.

Why was the broom late for homeroom?
He overswept.

What do you call two birds in love?
Tweethearts!

What do you call a theme park with only giraffes in it?
Giraffic Park.

What's a polar bear's favourite song?
"Ice, Ice, Baby."

Why did the vegetable call the plumber?
It had a leek.

What's a slice of bread's favourite name?
Rye-n.

Why do Santa's elves go to therapy?
To help their elf esteem.

Which hand is better to write with?
Neither, it's better to write with a pen.

Why did the math book look so sad?
Because of all its problems.

Who earns a living driving their customers away?

A taxi driver.

Why are ghosts such bad liars?
Because you can see right through them.

Why did the pony get sent to his room?
He wouldn't stop horsing around.

What kind of dinosaur loves to sleep?
A stega-snore-us.

What do you call a bear with no teeth?
A gummy bear.

Why can't you trust stairs?
Because they're always up to something.

What's orange and sounds like a parrot.
A carrot.

What do you call a fish with no eye?
Fsh.

What do you call a dog magician?
A labracadabrador!

What do cows do for fun?
They go to the moo-vies.

Why did Humpty Dumpty have a great fall?
To make up for his miserable summer.

What does a ghost call his true love?
His ghoulfriend.

What do you call a polar bear in Mexico?
Lost.

How do billboards talk to one another?
With sign language.

What's the strongest type of sea creature?
Mussels.

Why was the baby strawberry crying?
His mom was in a jam!

What did Venus say while flirting with Saturn?
"Give me a ring sometime."

What do they serve for breakfast on flights?
Plane bagels.

What do cats always wear when they go to bed?
Paw-jamas.

Why couldn't the obtuse angle get a job?
It was too bent out of shape.

Which superhero is a pro at hitting home runs?
Batman.

Why did Darth Vader turn off all the lights in the room?
He likes it on the dark side.

What's an astronaut's favourite meal of the day?
Launch.

What does a volcano say to its crush?
"I lava you!"

Why should you never give Elsa a balloon?
She'll let it go.

What do you call a duck who loves making jokes?
A wisequacker!

What did the pickle say to a pal who wouldn't stop complaining?
"Dill with it."

What do you call a long-nosed mammal who loves to garden?
A yardvark.

What did the buffalo say to his son when he went off to college?
Bison!

What did the Dalmatian say after she had a huge meal?
"That hit the spot."

What animal knows the metric system?
A centipede.

What do you call a band of berries practicing music?
A jam session.

What did one slice of bread say to the other during a fight?
"You're toast!"

Why do mushrooms get invited to all the parties?
Because they're such fun guys.

What did the cupcake tell its frosting?
I'd be muffin without you.

Why didn't the dog see a psychiatrist?
He isn't allowed on the couch.

What do Italian ghosts have for dinner?
Spookhetti!

What's a geologist's favourite place to bring a date?
A rock concert.

What does a storm cloud make sure to wear under her raincoat?
Thunderwear.

What is a dog's favourite Christmas song?
"Bark the Herald Angels Sing."

What do you call a cat who works in business?
A professional.

What did the loaf of bread write in a note to its sweetheart?
I loaf you!

How many lips does a flower have?
Tu-lips.

What are the strongest days of the week?
Saturday and Sunday. All the others are weekdays.

You walk into a bar and there is a long line of people waiting to take a swing at you.
That's the punch line.

How did one tectonic plate apologize to the other?
"My fault."

If they were to cast only dogs in movies, who would play Harry Potter?
Spaniel Radcliffe.

Which planet is the best singer?
Neptune.

What type of keys are known for being extra sweet?
Cookies!

Why did the teacher wear sunglasses to class?
Because his students were so bright.

Why did the crab refuse to share?
Because he's shellfish.

What dog can run really fast and cook a mean spaghetti dinner?
An Italian greyhound.

Why can't you tell a dog a knock-knock joke?
Because every time she hears knocking, she won't stop barking.

What's an apple's favourite way to fly?
Fruit flies.

Why did the loaf of bread decide to adopt a puppy?
It thought the puppy was a-dough-rable.

What do you call a guy who never farts in public?
A private tutor.

How do you get a tissue to dance?
You put a boogie in it.

Why do seagulls live by the sea?
Because if they lived by the bay, they'd be bagels!

How does a scientist freshen her breath?
With experi-mints!

What is a chicken's least favourite day?
Fry-day.

Why do the French eat snails?
They don't like fast food.

TEACHER JOKES

What do you say when two dogs have a crush on each other?
They caught the love pug.

What's a cat's least favourite jacket?
A fleas-lined coat.

Why did the dog cross the road?
To get to the barking lot.

Why did the gazelles forfeit the game?
The other team's players were all cheetahs.

What's the easiest way to identify carpenter ants?
By their tool belts.

What do you call a bird who plays sad songs on the guitar?
A blues jay.

What did the whale say when he bumped into the shark?
"Sorry! I didn't do it on porpoise."

What did the finger confess to the thumb?
"I'm in a glove with you!"

Why is an obtuse triangle always so frustrated?
Because it's never right.

Why can't a nose be 12 inches long?
Because then it would be a foot.

What do you call a pair of monkeys who share an Amazon account?
Prime mates.

What did the firefly say to her best friend?
"You glow, girl!"

Why did the melon jump into the lake?
It wanted to be a watermelon.

Why don't lamps ever sink when they're in water?
They are too light.

Why aren't unicorns great dance partners?
They have two left feet.

What kind of jobs do funny chickens have?
They are comedi-hens!

Why did the hamster quit his exercise routine?
He felt like he was just going in circles and not getting anywhere.

What was the Seal's favourite game show?
Seal or No Seal.

Why don't dogs play cards in the wild?
There are too many cheetahs out there.

Why don't kittens like online shopping?
They prefer cat-alogues.

Why did the peach buy deodorant?
To freshen up its pits.

What did the vegetable say to its love?
I love you from my head to-ma-toes.

What's the fastest country in the world?
Russia.

My friend is an expert reading maps.
He's a legend.

Why did the squirrel like my friend?
Because my friend is nuts.

What did the wolf say when the mice bit him?
Owwwww-ch.

What do you call a cat who runs the post office?
Post Meowster.

What do you call a cat who teaches at a university?
A purrfessor.

How do you know your dog is a genius?
You ask him, "What is two minus two?" and he says nothing.

Why do jumping spiders jump?
Because humans are scary.

Why could the elephant remember the tortoise's name so many years after they met?
He has turtle recall.

What do you call a polar bear in the desert?
Lost.

What do you call best buds who love math?
Alge-bros.

What does a spider wear to her wedding?
A webbing dress.

What's a sleeping dinosaur called?
A dino snore.

What is the most famous type of animal in the sea?
A starfish.

What kind of fruit do twins love the most?
Pears.

Where do hamburgers go if they want to go dancing?
A meatball.

Why did Mickey Mouse decide to become an astronaut?
He wanted to visit Pluto.

What type of music do balloons hate listening to?
Pop.

Why do all witches wear black?
So you can't tell which witch is which.

How did the phone propose to his girlfriend?
He gave her a ring.

What do lawyers wear when they go to court?
Lawsuits.

What's a bee's go-to haircut?
A buzz cut.

What did the little boat say to the yacht?
"Can I interest you in a little row-mance?"

Why is it sad that parallel lines have so much in common?
Because they'll never meet.

What's a cat's favourite comedy show?
Caturday Night Live.

What do you call a cat prom?
A Fur Ball.

Who gives cats the best presents?
Santa Claws!

Why do beets always win?
They are un-beet-able.

TEACHER JOKES

What's a turnip's favourite soda?
Root beer.

What's a vegetable's favourite kind of joke?
A corny joke.

Why did the slice of bread snuggle up in a blanket?
To get toasty warm.

What did the dalmatian say after lunch?
"That hit the spot!"

Did you hear about the cheese factory explosion in France?
All that was left was de Brie.

What type of markets do dogs avoid?
Flea markets!

What's worse than finding a worm in your apple?
Finding half a worm.

Why do bees have sticky hair?
Their honeycombs.

What state has the most streets?
Rhode Island.

How does a penguin build its house?
Igloos it.

What do you call an elephant that doesn't matter?
An irrelephant.

Where do sharks go on vacation?
Fin-land.

What did the alien say to the cat?
Take me to your litter.

What do you call a cat who loves to bowl?
An alley cat.

Why did the boy name his dog Ten Miles?
So he could tell his gym teacher he walked Ten Miles every day.

How do birds prepare for tests?
They don't—they just wing it.

What did the dachshund say to her crush?
I long for you.

What did the dolphin say to the other fish?
You need a porpoise in life.

Why was the Australian car in the driveway?
It dingo.

How does the man in the moon cut his hair?
Eclipse it!

TEACHER JOKES

How did the hamburger say "bye" to his side dish?
"Later, tots!"

What's fast, loud and tastes good with salsa?
A rocket chip.

Where do ghosts like to travel on vacation?
The Dead Sea.

What did the triangle say when he got mad at the circle?
"You're pointless!"

Why did two fours skip lunch?
Because they eight.

What do you call a sheep that has no legs?
A cloud.

Why was everyone shocked that I let my pup drive my car?
They had never seen a dog park before.

How can you tell if your dog is lazy?
He only chases parked cars.

Why did the traffic light turn red?
It had to change in the middle of the street.

When does a joke turn into a dad joke?
When it becomes apparent.

TEACHER JOKES

What kind of dog is most like a cat?
A purr-man shepherd.

What was the dog's job at the fancy hotel?
He was a Labra-doorman.

Why do artichokes fall in love so easily?
They have big hearts.

What should you add to broth to turn it into golden soup?
Fourteen carrots.

Why do golfers always bring an extra pair of pants with them?
In case they get a hole-in-one.

Why did the kid throw the butter out the window?
To see a butterfly.

What kind of tree fits in your hand?
A palm tree.

How do you throw a birthday party on Mars?
You planet.

When a bird needs to invest her money, what does she do with it?
Puts it in the stork market.

Where do Arctic foxes store their money?
In snow banks.

TEACHER JOKES

What did the cat say when it lost all its money?
"I'm paw!"

Why don't cats like house parties?
Too many cat-astrophes.

Why did the cat wear a tuxedo?
He was feline fancy!

Why was the cat afraid of the tree?
Because of its bark.

Why is it so hard for a leopard to hide?
Because he's always spotted.

What is a witch's favourite lesson at school?
Spelling.

What is the tallest building in the entire world?
The library, because it has so many stories.

What is the smartest state in America?
Alabama. It has four As and one B.

What state makes the most pencils?
Pennsylvania.

What are a ninja's favourite type of shoes?
Sneakers!

TEACHER JOKES

What did the policeman say to his belly button?
"You're under a vest."

What's a vegetable's favourite backyard game?
Cornhole.

Why did the slice of bread get sent home from school?
It was feeling crumby.

What did the bun do when its plans suddenly changed?
It rolled with it.

What's a piece of bread's least favourite chore?
Doing a loaf of laundry.

Why do dragons sleep during the day?
So they can fight knights!

Why did the student eat his homework?
Because his teacher told him it was a piece of cake!

What has more letters than the alphabet?
The post office.

What's a cat's favourite dessert?
A mice cream cone.

What's a cat's favourite jacket?
A purr coat.

Why do cats always beat dogs in video games?
Because they have nine lives.

How does a cat answer the phone?
"Meow may I help you?"

Why did the boy put his money in the freezer?
He wanted cold, hard cash.

Where does Spider-Man do his best research?
The World Wide Web.

What has thousands of ears but can't hear at all?
A cornfield.

What dog breed would Dracula love to have as a pet?
A bloodhound!

What happened when the shark tried online dating?
He was catfished.

What is the most polite kind of dinosaur?
A please-iosaur.

What's the smartest type of insect?
A spelling bee.

How did the koala get the job?
He had the best koalifications.

TEACHER JOKES

Why was the fruit busy on Friday night?
It had a date.

How do you address a pineapple princess?
Your pine-ness.

Did you hear about the population of Ireland?
It's Dublin.

What do you call a rich elf?
Welfy.

How do you talk to giants?
Use big words!

Why was the skeleton afraid of the storm?
He didn't have any guts.

Why was the bicycle lying down?
It was two-tired.

What did one hat say to the other?
"I'm going on a-head."

What sound does a witches car make?
Broom Broom.

My wife asked me if I could clear the kitchen table.
I had to get a running start but I made it!

I can't take my dog to the pond anymore because the ducks keep attacking him.
Guess that's what I get for buying a pure bread dog.

What kind of dog never throws anything away?
A hoarder collie.

What's a banana's favourite way to say thank you?
Thanks a bunch!

Why didn't the cat get promoted to management?
He had terrible littership skills.

Why is it annoying to watch TV with cats?
They keep paw-sing the show.

What's a paddlefish's favourite song?
"Row, Row, Row Your Boat."

What's a mockingbird's favourite movie?
Mean Girls.

Why were all the penguins laughing?
Because the emperor penguin had no clothes.

What do you call a lazy baby kangaroo?
A pouch potato.

What did the fish say when he swam into a wall?
"Dam!"

What do you get when you cross a centipede with a parrot?
A walkie-talkie!

What animal has three humps?
A camel with a backpack.

Why was the equal sign so humble?
Because it wasn't greater than or less than anyone else.

What's a math teacher's favourite season?
Sum-mer.

How do you make seven an even number?
Just remove the s.

Why couldn't the pony sing at her choir concert?
She was a little horse.

What kind of vehicle has four wheels and flies?
A garbage truck.

What do you call a funny mountain?
Hill-arious.

If a clock strikes 13, what time is it?
Time to get a new clock.

Why did the student do multiplication on the floor?
The teacher told them not to use tables.

TEACHER JOKES

What kind of photos will you find on a turtle's phone?
Shell-fies.

Why couldn't the bicycle stand up by itself?
It was two-tired.

What did the ocean say to the beach?
Nothing. It just waved.

Why wasn't the stadium hot after the game?
Because there were so many fans.

What do you call cheese that doesn't belong to you?
Nacho cheese!

How do you know the ocean is friendly?
It waves.

Why is Cinderella so bad at playing football?
She runs away from the ball.

What do you call the cat that gets caught by the police?
The perpetrator.

How do cats say 10/10?
Purrfect.

How does a cucumber become a pickle?
It goes through a jarring experience.

TEACHER JOKES

What do you call a fake noodle?
An im-pasta.

How do you make an artichoke?
You strangle it.

What did the left eye say to the right eye?
"Something between us smells!"

Why did the clock go to the principal's office?
For tocking too much.

What do you call a dishonest reptile?
A crookodile.

What do you call a broke Santa Claus?
Saint Nickel-less.

What does a pampered cow give us?
Spoiled milk.

What did the lion say to the deer?
"Pleased to eat you".

Why did the nose complain about the finger?
Because the finger was always picking on him.

Why are colds not good criminals?
Because they are very easily caught.

TEACHER JOKES

Why was the coffee scared?
He got mugged.

A traffic cop went to the trouble of putting a note on my windshield to let me know I positioned my car correctly.
It said 'parking fine' so that was nice.

Can February March?
No, but April May.

What should you say to a runner in the St. Patrick's Day marathon?
Irish you luck

What did the hipster say the day after Thanksgiving?
"I liked the leftovers before they were cool."

Why did the man get fired from the orange juice factory?
Lack of concentration.

What is a tornado's favourite game to play?
Twister!

What do music and chickens have in common?
Bach, Bach, Bach!

What did one penny say to another penny?
"We make cents."

Where do you take a boat with a cold?
The boat doc.

TEACHER JOKES

Why can't eggs tell jokes?
Because they'd crack each other up.

Why did the pod excuse itself from the dinner table?
It had to pea!

Why didn't the slice of bread laugh when someone told it a joke?
It was a little stale.

Why did the tomato blush?
Because it saw the salad dressing.

What did one plate whisper to the other plate?
Dinner is on me.

Why didn't the teddy bear eat dessert?
He was stuffed.

What is a tree's least favourite month of the year?
Sep-timber!

What's a pirate's favourite country to travel to?
Arrrgentina.

What do you get when you cross a fish and an elephant?
Swimming trunks.

What kind of fish travel in tiny cars?
Clownfish.

What do you get if you divide the circumference of a jack-o'-lantern by its diameter?
Pumpkin pi.

Why did the student get upset when their teacher called them average?
It was mean!

Why was trigonometry class so long?
The teacher kept going off on a tangent.

What's the most expensive fish?
A goldfish.

Why do so many fish live in salt water?
Because pepper water would make them sneeze.

What do bees brush their hair with?
Honeycombs.

What do you call a sleeping bull?
A bulldozer.

What starts with gas and has three letters?
A car.

Why did the kid throw his clock out the window?
To see time fly.

What's something that falls but will never hit the ground?
The temperature.

What's a computer's favourite thing to snack on?
Computer chips.

What candy is always running late to things?
Choco-late.

What's an alligator in a vest called?
An investigator.

Why did the chocolate chip cookie go to see the doctor?
He felt crummy.

What's a really sad strawberry called?
A blueberry.

What's one animal you'll always find at a baseball game?
A bat.

What's a pirate's favourite class to take in school?
Arrrt.

Why did the woman throw a ball for her dog?
Because it was his birthday, and he loves to dance.

What is a dog's favourite song to listen to after a bath?
"Shake It Off" by Taylor Swift.

What do you call a floating dog?
A good buoy.

When it's raining cats and dogs, what do you risk stepping in?
A poodle.

Why are border collies such good listeners?
Because you can tell they really herd you.

Which dog breed has never done anything wrong?
Saint Bernard.

Which type of dog is also a lamb?
A sheepdog!

Which dog is the quietest?
The Alaskan malamute.

What do you give a sick lemon?
Lemon-aid.

Why can't you trust atoms?
They make up everything.

How do you stop an astronaut's baby from crying?
You rocket!

What's red and smells like blue paint?
Red Paint.

What kind of music do mummies listen to?
Wrap music.

What street do ghosts haunt?
Dead ends.

How much does it cost a Neutron to buy groceries?
No charge.

What is very odd?
Every other number.

What is a cat's favourite colour?
Purrple.

What did the cat say to the dog?
"Meow-t of my way!"

What do you call a large dog that meditates?
Aware wolf.

What is a witch's favourite breed of dog?
A Yorkshire scarier.

Why shouldn't you buy essential oils from a cat?
It's probably a purr-amid scheme.

What is a pizza's favourite type of joke?
A cheesy one!

Why did the bird get in trouble in class?
He was tweeting on a test.

TEACHER JOKES

What do you call a pile of cats outside?
A meow-tain.

What's a math teacher's favourite plant?
A geometree.

What did the calculator say to her best friend?
"You can always count on me."

What's a pencil's favourite place to visit?
Pencil-vania.

What class do birds always ace?
Owl-gebra.

What's the best seat on a flight to a tropical vacation?
An isle.

What candy do bumblebees love the most?
Bumble gum.

What time is your dentist appointment?
Tooth hurty.

Why was the bullet unemployed?
Because it was fired.

What happened when David lost his ID?
He became Dav.

What did the big brother flower say to his little sister when she was born?
"Hi, bud".

I thought about going on an all-almond diet.
But that's just nuts.

Why can't you trust the king of the jungle?
Because he is always lion.

What do you call a fly without wings?
A walk.

What does a cow call his mother?
Moooo-m.

What happened to the toad who left the forest?
He was soon forgotten.

What was the first thing the baby corn asked the mama corn when he woke up?
"Where is pop corn"?

How do you make an egg roll?
Push it.

Why can't you put two half dollars in your pocket?
Two halves make a hole, so your money will fall out.

Which snakes are the best at math?
Adders.

What is black and white and red all over?
A penguin with sunburn.

What's a fruit's favourite motivational quote?
Seeds the day!

What did the fruit say to its best pal?
You're pretty grape.

What is a dog dentist's favourite tooth?
The canine.

Why was the dog such a good musician?
Because he had perfect "pooch."

What did the dad say when his daughter asked, "Have you seen the dog bowl?"
"No. I didn't even know he could play cricket!"

Why can't a man make milk?
Because he lactose qualities.

Whom can you always count on?
Your fingers.

Why do dogs howl at the night sky?
They get excited to see the bark side of the moon.

What kind of dog should you use to help unlock a door?
An A-key-ta.

What do you call a dog that does yoga?
A foldin' retriever.

What did the strawberry write to its crush?
I'm berry fond of you.

What book did the lime let the lemon borrow?
A Wrinkle in Lime.

Did you hear about the scarecrow who won first prize?
It was outstanding in its field.

What should you tell your family when they want you to stop telling Thankgiving jokes?
"I can't quit cold turkey."

I was going to take a hike in the snow yesterday.
But then I got cold feet.

What's a cat's favourite TV show?
Claw & Order: Special Kittens Unit.

Why did the cat cross the road?
To get to the other scratching post.

When is a door not a door?
When it's ajar.

Why did the picture get arrested?
It got framed.

What is the name of the penguin's favourite aunt?
Aunt Arctica.

How do you make an octopus laugh?
With ten-tickles.

Why is the keyboard always tired?
Because it has two shifts.

Why don't skeletons ever go trick or treating?
Because they have no body to go with.

Why did the invisible man turn down the job offer?
He couldn't see himself doing it.

What happens to a frog's car when it breaks down?
It gets toad away!

A vowel saves another vowel's life.
The other vowel thanks him, saying, "Aye E! I owe you!"

Printed in Great Britain
by Amazon